ZEN

FOR MODERN LIVING

ROY GILLETT

Published in 2001 by Caxton Editions
20 Bloomsbury Street
London WC1B 3JH
a member of the Caxton Publishing Group

Designed and produced for Caxton Editions
by Open Door Limited
Rutland, United Kingdom

Editing: Mary Morton
Illustration: Andrew Shepherd, Art Angle

Title: Zen
ISBN: 1 84067 285 4

IMPORTANT NOTICE

This book is not intended to be a substitute for medical advice or treatment. Any person with a condition requiring medical attention should consult a qualified medical practitioner or suitable therapist.

ZEN

FOR MODERN LIVING

ROY GILLETT

CAXTON EDITIONS

CONTENTS

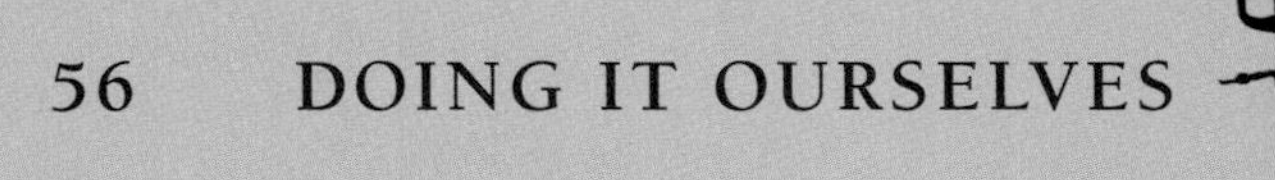

CONTENTS

WHAT IS ZEN?

Zen has one simple message – "things are as they are". Look at life in this way and all the regret, fear and envy that seem to plague us will fall away and the simple, clear wonder of reality will be revealed.

This is not the soft option it may seem at first. Seeing "things as they are" does not mean giving in weakly to brutality, or injustice, because we "cannot do anything about it". Quite the opposite – we stand firmly and calmly by the facts of the situation, without fear or favour for ourselves or anyone else. Nor does this mean a struggle for the truth. The Zen mind does not struggle – it sees.

Nor is it an excuse for inaction – "things are as they are, so nothing can be done". Again, quite the opposite – Zen practice abounds with skillful words and techniques to train the mind to perceive the clear light of truth, and let irrelevant attachments just fall away.

This is often illustrated with simple stories and actions. "A British university professor decided to visit a Zen Master to discuss the nature of existence. The Master welcomed him by offering a cup of tea. When the cup was full, he carried on pouring, until at last the professor felt obliged to point out the cup was full, no more would go in. To which, the Master replied, 'Like this cup, you are full of your opinions and theories. How can I show you Zen, unless you first empty your cup?'"

Left: Zen has one simple message – "things are as they are", once you are able to look at all life in this way, the clear wonder of reality will be revealed.

A Zen koan, a riddle that enlightens, is another way. "Listen to the sound of one hand clapping."

Teachings of wise masters are important. Chuang-tzu taught, "The perfect man employs his mind as a mirror. It grasps nothing: it refuses nothing. It receives, but it does not keep."

Right: the mind of a perfect man is as a mirror, "it grasps nothing: it refuses nothing. It receives but it does not keep."

Zen Buddhism developed in China and then Japan by combining Mahayana Buddhism from Northern India and Chinese Taoist philosophy.

Gautama Buddha lived between 500 to 600 years before Christ. He was born the son of a king, given every comfort and guarded from all the sufferings of life. On reaching manhood and seeing life as it really was, Gautama gave up everything to wander, meditate and finally discover, under the bodhi tree at Bodh Gaya, the essential suffering of ordinary existence and the means of liberation from this suffering.

Ordinary sense-based life is subject to unreliable change. Attachment to sensory things that will not last is the root of all suffering. We liberate ourselves from this by following a path of morality, generosity and fearless, objective clarity. The Mahayana branch of Buddhism emphasises that full understanding can only be achieved, if we act in a way that will bring happiness to everyone.

Left: a Japanese Buddha.

Below left: Gautama Buddha, born the son of a king, but gave up everything to wander and meditate

Taoism developed in the third century BC from a religious tradition based on the teaching of Lao-Zhu. Taoism teaches that society's rules should play a secondary role. Much more important is for each of us to seek unity with the underlying pattern of the Universe. This is called the Tao or "way". It cannot be explained in words, nor can it be struggled after. On the contrary – by emptying ourselves of all doctrines and knowledge – we see clearly the way things are. Then we become so in tune with the Tao, that we develop a power to act that many see as a magical force.

It is this Taoist way that lies at the heart of the various forms of Eastern martial arts – such as Kung Fu – that have become so popular in our modern world. When we use such skills for personal power, we may make temporary gains, but they will ultimately destroy us. When we use them for the benefit of everyone our strength and happiness increase.

Right: it is this Taoist way that lies at the heart of the various forms of Eastern martial arts – such as Kung Fu

Clearly, Zen is not an unrealistic retreat from the "world as it is". On the contrary, it offers us great strength and happiness and the ability to bring happiness to others and so create a better world for everyone. In the modern world, we spend much time yearning for what we cannot have, but feel we ought to have. Often we do not want what we do have. We argue for our "rights" and reject, sue and legislate against those we feel are denying them. Our entertainment and artistic culture centres on fear, jealousy, greed, disappointment, frustration, possessiveness, attachment to family and special "friends" and condemnation of "enemies". Usually, this is done, not to cut through these delusions to the clear light of truth that puts such counter-productive attitudes in perspective. It is done to celebrate the triumph of one view of "truth" over another. One norm becomes "good", its opposite becomes "evil". "Evil" must be made to suffer and then destroyed, so that "good" (the partial truth the character prefers) can be "enjoyed for ever". Zen teaches that yearning for such "solutions" rather than seeing things as they are causes everything that goes wrong in our lives. In short, we are straining to obtain what we do not want at all.

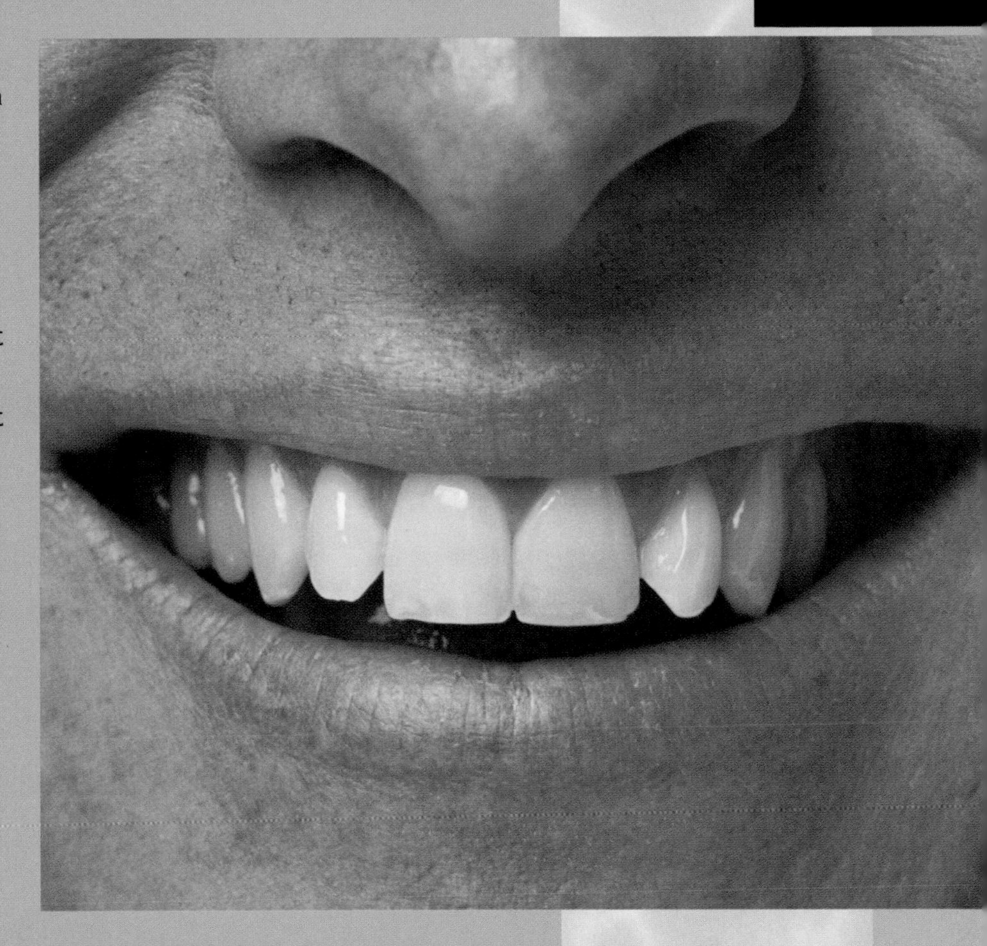

Above: Zen offers us great strength and happiness and the ability to bring happiness to others and so create a better world for everyone.

Above: once we get the knack of zen it has the ability to free us of stress naturally, leaving us happier and truly contented.

Developing a Zen view will give us a proper understanding of our situation, by clearing it of the clutter of personal emotion and prejudice and broadening what we take into account. Once we get the knack of it, finding solutions to problems can be free of stress. They can happen naturally, automatically – as if by magic.

Whether we are looking for a parking space, cooking a meal, deciding on a relationship, applying for a job, or kept hanging on the phone, applying a Zen approach can only enhance our lives in today's world. All Zen is saying is "find and enjoy what you really want" and "here are some simple methods to do just this".

Left: all Zen is saying is "find and enjoy what you really want".

IDEAL HOME

We are bombarded with suggestions telling us how to live "happily ever after" in our home. Particular objects, styles, colours go in and out of fashion conveniently in accord with the yearly retail cycle. So there is always something more to consider and include in our quest for the "Ideal Home".

Below: colours and styles go in and out of fashion on a yearly basis and we are continually bombarded with pressure to keep up with the latest ideas and styles.

As well as things to purchase there are all those jobs to be done. For, although we live in a busy world that keeps us away from our loved ones most of the week, whenever there is some spare time, it seems we should spend it improving the home.

The development of DIY shops with easy-to-use and apply products and the apparent commitment to them of our neighbours creates irresistible pressure. Should we use that, or this idea, or colour, or method, re-decorate entirely, have an extension, a conservatory, or re-surface the drive? Will it increase the value of the property and bring it up to the same standard or beyond the other houses in the street?

Whether we live like this or more modestly, problems of what to put in our homes and especially where plague our minds. For many of us, it is much easier to obtain new things than to let go of existing ones. So the home becomes increasingly full. Things just sit there, or fill our cupboards to bursting. We spend far less time considering exactly how often we use an object than we do obtaining and deciding where to put new ones.

Many of us develop fetishes that focus on particular possessions, which can take over our homes completely. Particularly dangerous are indoor plant and fish-tank enthusiasts. The home can seem like a humid jungle, with "factory" sounding machinery humming 24 hours a day. The television dominates room layout in most homes, so much so that it becomes self-confirming. Because the room is designed to watch television, people spend most of their leisure time doing just that.

Above: most living areas are designed around the television and result in most of the leisure time we have being taken up by watching it.

Left: the attraction of indoor plants to some people can result in the living areas resembling humid jungles.

Right: possessions have the ability of reflecting our whole lives, whether they are needed or not, we find a way to fit them in and we become reluctant to let go of them.

The reason we fall into one or more of the above traps is because we make piecemeal decisions about our homes and never get around to considering and deciding an overall plan. One of us brings something home. We find a way to "fit it in". Having "fitted it in" it becomes a part of our identity, which we are reluctant to let go of. In the end our possessions determine the quality of our lives, without us ever making a full reasoned decision that we really want things that way.

Right: on the opposite extreme, people can become paranoid about things being out of place or the occurrences of minor breakages.

Those of us who are determined not to fall into this trap can go to the other extreme of anxiously re-designing our home, so that everything is perfectly chosen and placed. This brings two new problems. The usually extended debate about placing and style choices can be anxious and nerve-wracking. In the midst of all this we tend to overlook the need to live in the home. So a magazine or item of clothing out of place, or a minor breakage can become major problems.

The first stage in solving all these problems is to put aside assumptions about what is and is not needed in the home. While keeping in the back of our minds all we know about our own and our family's needs, we should look at our home as a complete stranger would, if seeing it for the first time. Then sit down and relax, or do something entirely different – preferably something that has to be done – maybe prepare or eat a meal. Do not think, just let it all sink in. This second stage allows change to come spontaneously from within and to grow organically. We will need to discuss things, but not decide immediately. If the solution does not appear, put the problem to one side for a while. Good answers come, when we stop wanting them. As we develop the knack of this non-grasping approach, new ideas will emerge. We will find ourselves applying them and riding a natural surge of energy that seems to be rising up within us. When one home project is complete another may arise naturally. If it does not, do something else. Let the mind be blank for a while. Leave space for a new possibility to come. Discuss ideas, but do not struggle after solutions. It will ruin the magic of being in tune with the flow.

Above: when deciding on what changes to make, do something that needs to be done which is totally unrelated such as preparing a meal.

Right: an ideal home will emerge naturally without forcing an idea, and as you develop this non-grasping approach you will find new ideas revealing themselves and a natural flow will develop.

Below: Zen offers a way of making space in our minds by clearing the clutter and allowing us to realise the home we really want.

Unlike Feng Shui, Zen does not offer a detailed description of proper placing and action in accordance with the natural flow. Rather it offers a way of training the mind to let go of unnatural assumptions and attachments and so leave the space for what we know already in our deepest being to emerge and enrich our lives. This emergence is the magic we experience, when we allow the confusion and clutter to fall away from our minds. Resist nothing, permit the unthinkable – you can have the home you want.

Then, there are those times, when we know what we want, but circumstances prevent it. It may be that we cannot make the changes we wish. Maybe the landlord, or planning officer will not agree, the cost is too high, or we just do not have the time, or energy. Zen can help us through this "not doing". By acknowledging what we want, but cannot have, we can see clearly what we are missing and how the dissatisfaction surrounding this is distorting our lives. Two possibilities are open to us in these circumstances – leave our present situation for a more favourable one, or accept that other factors in our lives justify our staying. We bide our time, while clearly noting and measuring the disadvantages. In this way we prevent them confusing and spoiling the pleasure and spontaneity of our lives.

Above: sometimes, even when we have the right plans and know exactly what we want, circumstances do not allow us to put these ideas into action – Zen can help us deal with the disappointment of this.

SUCCESSFUL RELATIONSHIPS

"If you love someone set them free.
If they return, they are yours.
If they do not they never were."

It is so easy to take other people for granted and expect them to be like us and understand what we want. Then we feel let down, when they do something we dislike, or seem to be taking us for granted.

Below: dating can be such a let-down, but a Zen approach can help us to address problems as they arise.

Dating especially can be such a let down! We may have spent hours thinking about how we should make that first phone call. We may have acted carefully on advice from our favourite magazine and talked to friends. We may have rehearsed exactly what we should say, only to find the phone engaged, or be told the other person is too busy. If we do get past this first hurdle and we dress carefully to look our best, our date may seem to hardly look at us. If they do, they may not consider us as we expected. They may wish to go somewhere we do not like, be boring and talk about themselves all the time. Then, if everything goes perfectly, they do not make another date, but keep us "hanging on". Then we see them with someone else. We may start to wonder what we did wrong. If they are faithful to us, they may be reluctant to make long-term commitments, or on the other hand they may demand commitments, we do not feel ready to make. Even if we do agree on being committed to each other, we may discover that our tastes differ widely and things we have been willing to "put up with" earlier in the relationship will need to change if we are to live together. On the other hand, we may feel put upon and controlled, so we have lost our independence and ability to make our own decisions.

Left: the more we feel the need for another person the more vulnerable we are to things going tragically wrong.

The Zen way to avoid these various disappointments is not to try, but rather to look at and handle each situation appropriately. By focussing on our own needs, rather than those of another person and the total situation, we may misunderstand, cause embarrassment and put ourselves impossibly in the wrong. The more we feel we need another person, the more tragically dangerous this can become – right up to the horrors depicted in the film *Fatal Attraction*.

Below: demands to possess or control are not love. true love grows in wonderfully surprising ways all the time.

In the modern world, we speak a lot about the importance of "love", but less often consider what it means.

Someone may say, "You cannot leave me – I love you!" This is not love at all. If we really love someone, the first thing we wish for is his or her happiness. Whether our lover cares for us whatever happens is the crucial test of true love. Demands to possess, or control another's movements are not "love".

This distinction is absolutely crucial. When our lover cares for our needs, we feel safe with them. Everything we do together restores our faith in each other. Sexual interactions occur naturally. We do not need friends or therapists to guide us. We know it is right, because our love grows in wonderfully surprising ways all the time, until we are so sure that nothing can change how we feel.

Marriage can bring new dangers of disappointment. There are two main causes, which tend to reinforce each other. Once married, most people are more likely to buy property and other possessions and have children. These joint responsibilities build up and demand such long-term effort and routine that the relationship is taken for granted. Although bound by so many "obligations", the couple can find they are drifting apart and no longer enjoy their time with each other. The marriage becomes no more than going through the motions with dulled, unaware eyes.

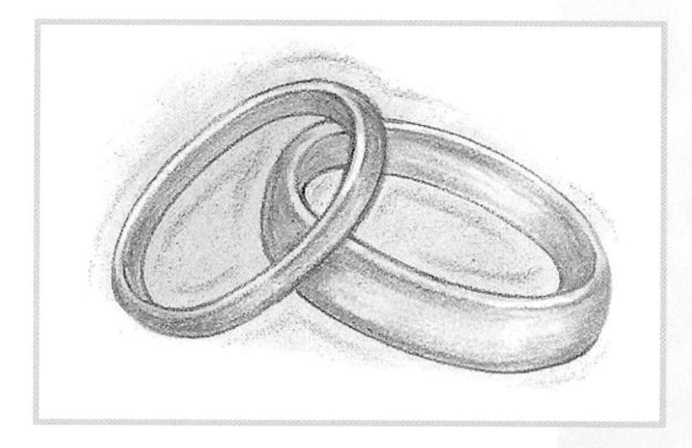

To avoid this, it is crucial for each partner to keep a fresh Zen perspective in their individual lives and, at the same time, ensure the other experiences ongoing fulfilment, support and encouragement. This need not be impossibly idealistic, or mean "living in each other's pocket". It is just a continuation of the love and concern that characterised the early stage in the relationship. "I am I and you are you and if by chance we meet it is beautiful" can be just as true in a marriage, where two people spend much of their day apart, as it was at the beginning of the relationship. It is just as productive for each to see the other work hard and succeed in life. When the relationship is dedicated to the world in this way, the couple will never be apart.

Left: Once married, it is crucial for each partner to keep a fresh Zen perspective in their lives.

Right: "I am I and you are you and if by chance we meet it is beautiful" can be just as true in a marriage, where two people spend much of their day apart, as it was at the beginning of the relationship.

In traditional cultures, the old are the wise custodians of the tribal culture – they are always consulted and make the important decisions. If we turn to and listen to our older people, we could enjoy similar benefits and they their lives. The way of Zen is to hear what is said, not judge and reject it in advance. When we guide a rambling explanation back to its centre, we draw out the meaning of the core for the benefit of everyone. When we draw knowledge from an ever-wider range of people and experiences, we enhance the depth and strength of our understanding and increase the effectiveness of our actions.

Above: old people looking for a role in life and waiting for the next Sunday visit are sad, all too common, images in today's modern society.

Older people confront us with one of the most painful paradoxes in living today. Most of us are staying alive far longer than at any time in the past, yet western society is more and more geared towards the young. Today, it can be difficult to find a "proper job" beyond our forties. The old person rambling on irrelevantly about the past, or cosy grandparents desperately looking for a role in life and waiting for the next Sunday visit are sad, all too common, images.

Right: if we turn to and listen to our older people, we could enjoy similar benefits to traditional cultures who regard the old as custodians of tribal culture.

Giving presents and the manipulation surrounding this giving is a major industry in today's world. At heart, the intention is excellent. We wish to surprise someone and make them happy, but why? Is it so they will like us? Are we motivated by guilt? Do we want to put them under some obligation? Are we looking for a better present in return? If so, then the gift will be tainted. We are not really giving at all, rather seeking to take from the "recipient".

In our materialistic modern world, we have to ask who is the real gainer from the gift? Very often it is the manufacturer, retailer, or the promotion team. The advertising revenue gained by the television or magazine company can be used to produce lowest common denominator mass-audience programmes. By giving a gift we may well be starting a chain of dysfunctional commerce. In which case our giving is really harming the loved recipient of the gift, as well as many other people.

Below: in our materialistic modern world, we have to ask who is the real gainer from a gift?

In Buddhist cultures, people "of good family" train their minds by making altar offerings in a very special way. In such giving, we let go of any sense of loss or gain and release our minds completely from attachment to what we previously possessed. It is now given. This brings two benefits. It teaches us how to let go. It purifies our mind from the pain and confusion of expectation and imposing obligations on others. In fact, such pure generosity can lead to great gains in the future, but only if we put aside all expectation. Understanding this paradox is the major skill needed to learn true generosity.

Right: purifying our mind of the pain and expectation when dealing with gifts allows the possibility of pure generosity, without obligation.

Captivated by a celibate Buddhist teacher, a young woman sat through all his teachings and finally plucked up the courage to arrange a personal interview with him. Knowing it was considered beneficial to give to the teacher, she prepared the most beautiful bouquet of flowers, offered them with great affection and then sat opposite him, hanging on his every word, anxiously waiting to see his response to her gift. Surely she would become his favourite student! The teacher put the flowers gently to his side and turned away from them without looking back. He asked where she lived and if she had any questions. Confused, she found herself talking about mistakes she had made in life. As the conversation proceeded, she noticed he had, as if without thinking, taken one of the flowers from its bundle and was aimlessly picking off the petals as he listened. At this point, she felt released from the pain of regret she felt for many of the failures and negative actions in her life.

Above left: an understanding of Zen enables you to release the pain of regret like picking off the petals on a flower.

Right: in Buddhist cultures, people "of good family" train their minds by making altar offerings in a very special way.

CHILDREN AND ADOLESCENTS

"Your children are not your children.
They are the sons and daughters of life's longing for itself."
Kahlil Gibran, The Prophet

In today's modern world, nothing stirs emotions and opinions more than issues surrounding the care and protection of children and the problems of adolescents.

The decades since the birth of the older members of our society have seen dramatic changes in attitude and practice. Regimes of strict discipline based on dictums such as "spare the rod and spoil the child", "children should be seen and not heard" and "the woman's place is in the home" predominated until the early 1960s. The older generation presided over what seemed to be moral and ordered societies. Only today has the truth about the brutality and abuse of children by individuals in some of the world's most respected institutions been revealed. Since the 1960s a radical change in values, leading to child-centred education, child protection and children's rights has developed. Today, even a parent striking a child in corrective love, let alone a teacher doing so, risks being considered an abuser by most people. Education is organised with anxious determination to give benefit and opportunity to every child. Teachers are constantly checked and badgered to ensure they are not falling down on the job. Society is expected to discover and correct the failings of poor parents. Products and advertisements targeted at children are lucrative businesses.

Right: there have been dramatic changes in child-care over recent years and the dictum of "children should be seen and not heard", is now happily unfashionable.

Left: since the 1960s a radical change in values, leading to child-centred education, child protection and children's rights has developed.

In spite of this turnaround, stories of child abuse and assault dominate our news. Child helplines are overwhelmed. Many parents are more frightened to let their children wander than in the past. For all the wealth and opportunity in our modern world, the adolescents, in particular, seem no happier. They need to consume great quantities of alcohol then disrupt and damage towns at night. Even younger children can become vandals and thieves and terrorise their neighbourhoods. Over the past 50 years have we moved on from terrorising our children to rearing children that will terrorise us? Does Zen offer a more stable way of handling the upbringing of new generations?

Right: the adolescents seem no happier with this new age of care. They consume great quantities of alcohol and make noise and damage towns at night.

Left:the Zen cure for unhappiness in children and adolescents would be to return to an interactive balance between "work" and "food".

A Zen master worked in the garden every day until his eighties. Feeling he should not work at his age, his pupils hid away his tools. For three days he did not eat. Feeling he was angry with them, the pupils returned his tools. The next day the master worked and ate. Later he taught them, "No work, no food". This simple story reveals the error of both the earlier and modern approaches toward children and adolescents. In the earlier approach, they were seen as cheap labour – much work, little food. Today we give them more and more – little work, too much food. Children reared under the earlier regime have overcompensated in the rearing of their own children. The Zen cure would be to return to an interactive balance between "work" and "food".

Bringing up children requires one fine judgement after another, but this guiding principle of what the child is expected to give and take can clarify these decisions. Realising that it is only by mastering this balance that the child can become a stable and happy adult should release the parent from guilty feelings of "not doing or giving enough". Having this yardstick also makes it easier to be generous and loving – to stretch the rules a bit.

Right: when a baby is a newborn a loving parent will meet its every demand instantly

Below: as a baby develops it will learn to sit up and move around by itself.

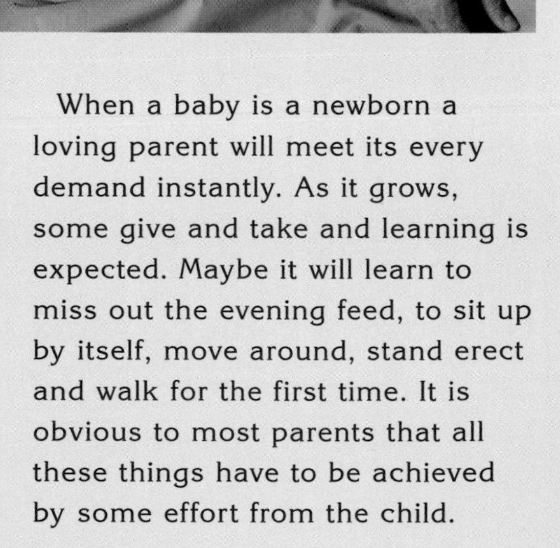

When a baby is a newborn a loving parent will meet its every demand instantly. As it grows, some give and take and learning is expected. Maybe it will learn to miss out the evening feed, to sit up by itself, move around, stand erect and walk for the first time. It is obvious to most parents that all these things have to be achieved by some effort from the child.

Then comes learning to relate to others, to help, to study, to do without and the give and take of receiving and giving presents. In school, the relative efforts of teacher and child need to have balanced expectations.

Left: learning to relate to others is another step in the development of a child.

Having the desired possessions and entertainment and how they are paid for become increasingly vital issues, as the child grows into adolescence.

At each stage, the area of parental responsibility is reduced and the area increased, where the adolescent must earn what they want for themselves. There will be errors, abuses and disappointments. Anxiety over this is difficult to avoid, but if love and respect can be sustained, a kind responsible adult will emerge from the process.

Left:at each stage, the area of parental responsibility is reduced and the area increased , where the adolescent must earn what they want for themselves.

PREPARING AND ENJOYING A GOOD MEAL

Compared to other animal species, human beings living in the more affluent areas of the world have a very distant relationship with their environment. The way we shop for and prepare our food is a prime example.

Traditionally, the harvest was the crucial communal event in everyone's year. Most people had played a part in its sowing and reaping. Also people were much closer to the slaughter of animals. With little refrigeration, storage for consumption through the lean times needed to be a long, careful process. It was vital to know what would be available in each season and organise accordingly. Today, most kinds of food from all over the world are available all the year round. We can store perishable foods for many months and use them when we wish. If that were not easy enough, we have the option to purchase many kinds of ready-prepared meals – some quite luxurious – and just heat and eat them within a few minutes in a microwave oven.

Right:Traditionally, the harvest was the crucial communal event in everyone's year. Most people had played a part in its sowing and reaping.

Left: the sheer range of immediately available food choices can lead to a basic sense of indifference, taking what we have for granted, or a hypercritical obsession with style and quality.

Yet, all these wonderful conveniences do bring their problems. Too much use of modern chemistry in the various stages of food production has proved to be dangerous – the effects of insecticides and the BSE crisis are well-known examples. In spite of more availability and improved knowledge of nutrition and the effects of various foods, fatty, carbohydrate-dominated diets are still favoured by far more people than is good for the health of society. The sheer range of immediately available food choices can lead to a basic sense of indifference, taking what we have for granted, or a hypercritical obsession with style and quality. How can Zen clear a way through all this and help us do the shopping and prepare a good meal?

Right: the Zen approach to food can result in a true adventure: the pleasure of which is not just in the journey of the preparation, but in the enjoyment of the "arrival" and eating of the meal.

Simple Zen methods for cutting through uncertainty hold the key. A novice monk once asked the Master to tell him how to study Zen. The Master replied by asking: "Have you eaten?"
"Yes, Master, I have eaten well, thank you."
"Then go and wash your bowl."

Preparing to shop for the week at a large modern supermarket can be a nightmare of truly frightening proportions. How do we list and find all we need and (with all those carefully labelled prices and weights) perform the arithmetic to make sure we do not "pay too much"? When we arrive, how do we resist the many temptations and offers and stop ourselves being tempted by packaging into buying what we do not need? The crucial thing is to do what it feels right to do next and refuse to be intimidated by expectations and anxiety over matters that are not yet problems. When we are preparing to shop, we should do just that. Make a rough list, knowing it will not include everything, but will have most of the essentials. When we are in the supermarket, we go through the shop quickly picking what we know we want. Allow a little spontaneous buying. We will notice what we really need almost popping into our hand. Do not be too dominated by price, or special offers, unless we really want them. When we get into the Tao (the way) of shopping, it seems as though there is a magic hand guiding our choices – the shopping does itself.

When preparing and cooking our purchases, there is more to life than a quickly oven-heated luxury frozen pizza, a freshly boiled plate of noodles, fried or oven-baked chips and barbecued burgers and sausages. Even the most exotic factory-prepared microwave meal can be surpassed by a little kitchen Zen.

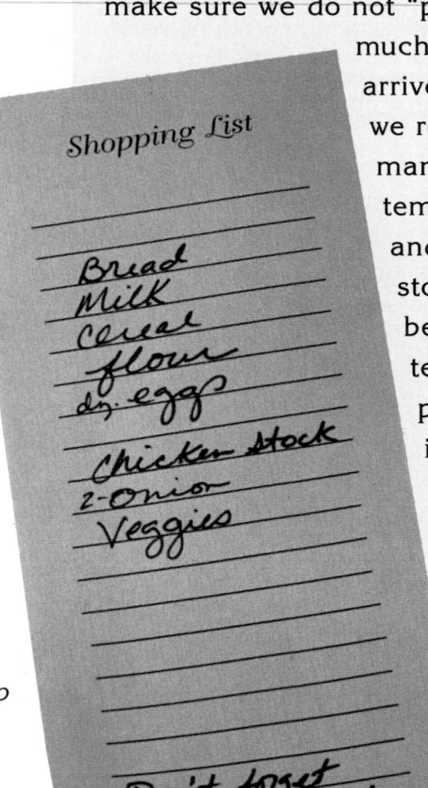

Right: when preparing to shop for food, make a rough list, knowing it will not include everything, but will have most of the essentials.

We must keep the image of the novice monk washing his bowl in our minds. Everything in its place in good time. Firstly, we look through the cupboards to see what is available. Often the items that are most in need of using up, when combined with others and a little imagination, will make the best meal. A waste-free kitchen is a good kitchen. With the ingredients laid out in front of us, we could then turn to and follow a recipe, but quite often I find that a meal suggests itself just by looking at the ingredients. Rather like a sculptor helping the sculpture emerge from a solid piece of material, so a Zen cook can combine ingredients to produce a tasty and nourishing meal. We develop a relationship with the nature of the food, the heat, the flavouring and the presentation.

Timing is the final and most magical ingredient. Again this should emerge from the natural flowing relationship we have with the ingredients and what we are trying to do. While a "watched pot never boils", over-cooking can boil out all flavour, or destroy texture. The middle way that emerges naturally from our sensitive understanding and relationship with the ingredients, utensils, heating and motions of our cooking art creates a delicious meal. Usually the process starts with slow and deliberate steps, but it can build to a stimulatingly hectic, but still controlled climax. An adventure indeed: the pleasure of which is not just in the journey of the preparation, but in the enjoyment of the "arrival" and eating of the meal.

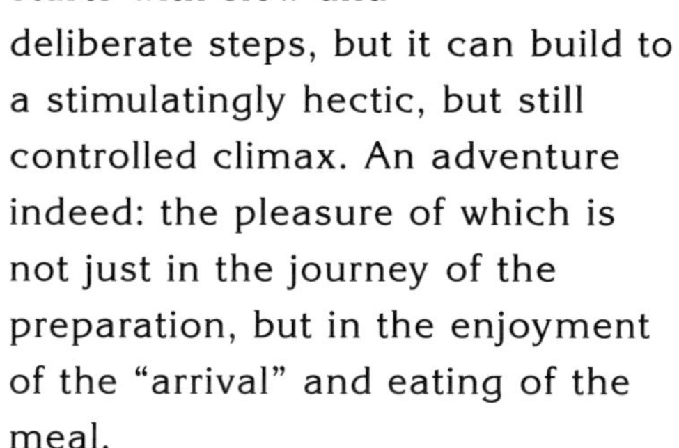

Bon appetit!

ENJOYING THE GARDEN

Below: today, when so many facts of modern living separate us from the natural world, it is our gardens that can keep us in touch with our animal roots.

"Sitting quietly,doing nothing,
Spring comes and the grass grows by itself."
The Zenrin

Whether we complain about how frequently the grass needs cutting in the summer, spend every spare minute out there pottering about, or do not have a garden at all, our relationship with gardening is the closest most of us come to nature in the modern world.

Increases in the size and number of garden centres and the dominance of garden programmes on prime-time television is a clear sign of the interest busy working people have in the green-fingered arts. Why this attraction? After a hard week's work, the last thing we would expect is for people to plan a weekend of more hard labour. We struggle to and through busy macro markets, dig heavy earth, bend, lift, cut and carry until late into the evening. Then we go to work after the weekend, are not there to enjoy our handiwork, until we find there is more work to do the next weekend.

Left: many questions arise from our activities in the garden; is the garden allowed to live and breathe, or are things just put in their place to fit neatly into our precisely planned display?

The attraction of cultivation and gardening is indeed ancient. From the time humanity ceased to rely solely on hunting and gathering, we have been tinkering with and trying to "improve" the wild reality of nature. Arguments for and against the supremacy of nature and man's nurturing of it have troubled philosophers. They even dominated the plot and imagery of Shakespeare's play *A Winter's Tale*. Today, when so many facts of modern living separate us from the natural world, it is our gardens that can keep us in touch with our animal roots.

In the garden, we are confronted constantly by decisions that question our right to interfere, or the wisdom of doing so. To what extent is the beauty we seek created by our leaving a plant's nature to emerge, or by intervening with modern chemicals and machinery that kill off the plant's enemies and tidy it up "ship shape" to fit neatly into our precisely planned display? Is the garden allowed to live and breathe, or are things just put in their place? Does what we do bring out and celebrate natural beauty in a comfortable environment, or just act as a pretty picture display created and sustained by artificial means?

One of the most telling tests is our attitude towards slugs, snails, other garden pests and "weeds" that just will grow where we do not want them! Garden centres abound with instant remedies to all such problems. However, such remedies bring with them several problems. By killing one pest we may be destroying friendly plants and creatures and creating an environment where an even worse pest can prosper. Even if the remedy has no side effects, the plant may seem too good to be natural – why not plant plastic flowers? If the plant we are protecting is for consumption, will the pesticide harm our family or us? As a result of the power of modern chemistry and genetics, it may take several generations of statistical survey to know the full effects of much of our interfering with nature.

Above: how we impose our ideas on our gardens shows whether we are at one and comfortable with our lives, or at war with our environment.

Gardens vary greatly between these two extremes and, in doing so, say much about the minds and emotional state of their creators. The way we impose ourselves upon nature in our garden and the reason we do shows whether we are at one and comfortable with our lives, or at war with our environment.

Left: when we live and work with the force and flow of nature, we find peace and the power of companionship.

In contrast to all this interference stands the Zen quotation at the head of this chapter. Is Zen really saying "Do nothing – do not garden at all"? Not necessarily and not not necessarily either! Crucial to everything is to know that there is a force and flow to nature that exists and continues. When we stand and fight against it, we lose our peace of mind and natural strength. When we live and work with the force and flow of nature, we find peace and the power of companionship. Then our garden becomes much more important than a mere object of pride, it becomes our home and increasingly a place of safety and joy. This is why details from nature so often decorate books of Zen sayings and teachings.

Right: our garden becomes much more important than a mere object of pride, it becomes our home and increasingly a place of safety and joy.

Below: by interacting with plants and creatures as if they are an intelligent part of our relationship pattern, we train our minds to see and act with clear understanding of what is needed.

Not that the Zen of gardening suggests we spend all our lives sitting there, while the weeds choke and dominate and "pests" devour. Rather that, as Zen gardeners, we act like loving parents to all of creation, gently adjusting and enabling all our "children" to grow and flourish. Many people smile with disbelief when they hear the British Prince of Wales say he talks to the plants in his garden, but it does make sense. They may be able to understand. Even if they do not, by interacting with plants and creatures as if they are an intelligent part of our relationship pattern, we train our minds to see and act with clear understanding of what is needed. If we experiment with this technique, we will see its value. Reflect the energy of wasps back to them, as one would to a recalcitrant child. Do not try to swat them. Instead form waves of air around their immediate environment to confuse their wings and make them fly away. Nothing wants to stay in an inhospitable environment, but every creature will defend itself against its attacker – especially, when it feels vulnerable and is about to die.

In our gardens, we try to find an appropriate place for the strength and colour of most things. The Japanese technique of creative pruning to sculpture bonsai trees naturally, made famous in the film *Karate Kid*, is typical of Zen gardening. Plants which some would call weeds can form a natural background, or even foreground, yet, if they dominate other plants, they can be cut back and contained. Put up natural barriers that guide and direct, rather than destroy pests – egg shells or dry gravel for slugs. We sit and study nature to learn. We companion plant, to encourage creatures that restrain what threatens our displays. We are as inclusive as possible.

To enter and sit in a truly Zen garden engenders a natural hush, a sense of being uplifted and safe – yet also a feeling of devotion, responsibility and care. This garden has not been created by brutality and ignorance. Everything there feels accepted and feels it is a part of something very precious.

Above: Zen gardening encourages plants and animals which put up natural barriers against pests.

Right: your garden does not need to be like this Zen rock garden to fulfil the the Zen ideas. To enter and sit in a truly Zen garden engenders a natural hush, a sense of being uplifted and safe – yet also a feeling of devotion, responsibility and care.

DOING IT OURSELVES

"Things in themselves have virtue.
Name them according to how and where they work.
When things are as they are, the lid fits the box.
Realising essence is like arrowheads meeting in mid-air."
From One and Many Engaged, by Shitou Xiqian

Around the corner, next door, or even in the same complex as the garden centre is the even more popular Do It Yourself supermarket.

DIY is a major way we cope with one of the major paradoxes and problems of our modern western world. We have developed social attitudes and techniques that enable a large proportion of our population to enjoy many of the comforts reserved for an exclusive few, until less than a hundred years ago. At the same time, there is not the space, nor the cheap labour that kept the aristocracy of the Victorian and earlier times in their splendour. As labour became more costly and materials less available, especially in the period after the Second World War, traditional methods of building were simplified and cheaper artificial, or recycled waste materials developed. Today most building techniques have become so simple that a reasonably strong person, with some bargain-priced power tools, can do most of the work around the home.

Right: today most building techniques have become so simple that a reasonably strong person, with some bargain-priced tools, can do most of the work around the home.

Today, we mend things, for which we would previously have called out an expert. What a chore this can seem.

The tap keeps on dripping, because we keep on forgetting to buy a washer and how can you find the correct one without turning off the water and taking it to the retail plumbers? Then there is that hinge that keeps on breaking and we have lost our screwdriver. Life can be so irritating! We are just about to go to bed, when the bulb goes on the landing and the baby will not sleep in total darkness, or in the bright light of its room! We are just about to serve a meal, when a blown fuse plunges the kitchen and dining room into darkness.

The Zen solution to a constant process of these and similar problems is to incorporate the maintenance and obtaining of resources for our home into the general pattern of our lives. We do not resent it, rather embrace and celebrate it as a broader dimension that enriches and completes our life experience. Ensuring a supply of light bulbs, washers, fuse wire and a tool kit are in and kept "in stock" becomes as natural as breathing and shopping. Rather than being annoyed, when something is missing, we see it as the chance to complete our supplies. So, when a job needs doing, we can take it up immediately in the flow. If eating the meal cannot wait, then using that candle that has stood virgin-like on the sideboard for a year or more could be a romantic change and just what is needed to change that display. If placed in a properly protected bowl, it might serve the baby's needs. This way we see not having light as enjoyable and a part of the process of having light.

Providing the resources for these odd jobs and more major projects has grown into a multi-billion pound world-wide DIY business. We are encouraged to tinker constantly with new objects, styles, paints and designs. The shape and uses of rooms are changed. Colour schemes are anxiously pondered over. Exotic names for shades and styles, constantly new fashions, bargain offers that cannot be resisted all build the tension of decision. For many people, a sense of proportion can go out of the window, when the need to decorate flies in. Noticing that neighbours are improving their homes again; needing to "increase the value of our investment"; being "unable to stand looking at that any longer" all fuel a need to act and fan the flames of "Ideal Home" hyperactivity.

Right: today's multi-billion pound world business encourages us to tinker constantly with new objects, styles, paints and designs.

Actually doing the work can bring further problems. Tools and materials cost money. Most people with a reasonable income work full time. So DIY has to be fitted in at weekends, in the evening, or even during the holidays. Living in a muddle with too much to do is not the best way to fit into the flow of what is for many not their normal kind of work. While professional people are repeating processes they learnt and mastered earlier in their career, many DIY people are learning on the job. So, most of these are unlikely to become experts, until they have finished the job – maybe not even then! For some, the experience of mastering something new is so exhilarating that they cannot wait to start the next task. They become enthusiasts, who are constantly looking for new things to do around the home. Those who do not are very likely to have forgotten and have to re-learn it all, when the next time comes around.

While we should recognise them, we should not be put off by these possible problems. Creating greater convenience, harmony, flow and beauty in our living environment can clear the mind and enhance our relationships. Enabling and releasing the possibilities of our home can enrich our family life and everything our family members touch and do. If we start from and stay with this perspective, rich benefits will flow from our work.

Left: While professional people are repeating processes they learnt and mastered earlier in their career, many DIY people are learning on the job.

Right: deciding what to do can be resolved by the usual Zen technique of staying with the problem without attachment to its difficulties and allowing the solution to emerge.

There are three possible problems.

Firstly, there is the anxiety of deciding exactly what to do and how. This can be resolved by the usual Zen technique of staying with the problem without attachment to its difficulties and allowing the solution to emerge. To decorate a room, some friends spent the first weekend checking over colour, furnishing and lighting possibilities and just bought one candleholder. This continued for a second one, leading to them buying an art déco lamp. They placed these in key positions in the new room and during the following week, all the ideas for decorating and furnishing the room fitted into place. They still maintain it is the best piece of creative DIY they have done. So much so, that the ideas developed for that room formed the foundation for the re-decoration of the whole house. What could have seemed to be an irritating "waste of time" ended up saving much time and money and producing the desired environment.

Secondly, avoid developing the habit of changing for change's sake, or depending on the judgement of others. It is not what we spend, or others think that is vital in the end. We have to live there. If the raison d'être of our lives is DIY, then we can continue this way happily. If not, then we should hold up the decision until we are satisfied with the flow. We should always remember we will be living there.

Left: avoid developing the habit of changing for change's sake, we should always remember we will be living there.

Thirdly, we have to keep our minds and relationships in good condition, while doing the work. We cut through negative states of mind, when we remember why we are doing the work. If it is for the sheer fun of it, there is no cause for complaint. If we are accepting inconvenience for a greater convenience later, then this should keep us going – even if the project turns out to be more demanding than expected. We have to work through it as pleasantly as possible – just as in a crisis, or great danger, we calmly do the best we can to extricate ourselves. Problems are most likely if we are trying to impress, or answer the demands of others. In such circumstances, we can only turn anger to ironic amusement, as we recognise the cause of our dissatisfaction and see ourselves suffering the consequences. Positive patience always brings great rewards.

Above: while doing the work, cut through negative states of mind, by remembering why we are doing the work.

In the end, all will change and fade away. If we do not believe this, all we need to do is scrape back through all the various colours and/or paper styles, with which the room has been decorated, or altered in the past. When we find ourselves restoring a room back to how it was in the beginning, we see the irony of all that energy devoted to decorating over the years. Learning to enjoy the intrinsic nature of where we are and the natural flow of the doing is always much more likely to satisfy, than any pattern book, or new fashion.

Left: learning to enjoy the intrinsic nature of where we are and the natural flow of the doing is always much more likely to satisfy, than any pattern book, or new fashion.

TRAVELLING AROUND

"If you don't see the path that meets your eye,
how will your feet know the way?
Moving forward isn't a question of near or far.
When you are lost, mountains and rivers block your way."
From One and Many Engaged, by Shitou Xiqian

Below: simply moving around in today's modern world can create stresses which can be helped by a Zen approach.

However familiar and comfortable we are with our home and family relationships, when we leave them we are likely to find a world of myriad beliefs, attitudes and practices, populated by people who know little or nothing about Zen.

Cars race past, cutting into our path. Sensing injustice and dangerous driving, we want to chase after and "teach them manners and some commonsense". We cannot find a parking space. The parking machine does not work. Do we dare risk being clamped? People push in front of us in queues. No one nowadays seems to know whether to walk on the left or right in public corridors, or staircases. A phone rings and interrupts our being served, clerks chatter aimlessly, computer keyboards demand ever-increasing input. We wait and feel the pressure of the queue lengthening behind us. As a result, we feel obliged to rush through our needs, so that we (or others) do not miss our vital train, or appointment. Putting everything back into our wallet seems to take forever, then the barrier does not work – heaven help the railway worker standing inactively by!

Flight booking queues can be nightmare cultures. Many seem designed to initiate us into accepting frustration, cramped spaces and being dependent on symbolic gestures. In such situations, the actions of others can play on our minds excessively. Is preventing queue jumping, or worrying about which is the fastest moving queue the best way to cope? When things go really wrong, how can we accept the lack of information, which seems like a long aching barrier of impossibility? Waiting strapped in a dimly lit space, delayed before take off at the end of the runway can seem like an endless time in limbo.

Above: everything about travelling around seems to be dominated by machines and automation, the human touch has become very difficult to find.

Entering and moving around public buildings can be a major challenge. Security passes, swipe cards and codes separate the wanted from the unwanted. Even reception staff can seem formal and unyielding. The human touch becomes increasingly difficult to find. Machines dispense our tickets, drinks and food – even decide whether we should enter a toilet or not. Surely there is no way Zen can help us through this kind of unnatural environment.

Start by realising that, for all its high-powered electronic and mechanical facilities, the essential nature of today's world "out there" is no different from many parts of nature. Equatorial jungles have even more difficulties and dangers. We have to master where we choose to live, or we will not be happy. Happiness comes by having the clarity and especially the patience to see all the time the essential nature of where we are and what we are doing.

Right: the essential nature of today's world "out there" is no different from many parts of nature. Equatorial jungles have even more difficulties and dangers.

From this way of looking, we will see true nature, structure, flow and, most importantly, the spaces, where our actions and needs fit in most easily.

Driving on the roads does require super awareness of future difficulties and quick reactions – so does the way of the zebra, travelling through the wild. Like it, we must find our way quickly, smoothly and quietly. Only very occasionally does the flow of Dharma, the Tao, require us to teach others. Usually, it is better to be patient and adjust. The Tao will find far better ways to teach. Road rage usually requires at least two participants. Finding a parking space is an art of cosmic timing. I go as close as I can to my destination. One will be there, if I am really in tune with the flow. It can be rather like surfing on the crest of a wave. If this does not work, I move intuitively away, trying to re-gain the flow. Seeing every failure to find a space as a lesson takes us to where we should be. The best bargain shoes I ever bought came from a shop found by dealing with parking restrictions in this way.

Above: driving on the roads does require super awareness of future difficulties – so does the way of the zebra, travelling through the wild. Like it, we must find our way quickly, smoothly and quietly.

Arriving in good time, relaxing into the pace of a delay (if it cannot be avoided) can bring many blessings, new friends, a book finished – very occasionally a life-saving adjustment to our journey. If we cannot avoid being trapped in impossible situations, we are pleased to do whatever we can to make them possible – who knows what magic, they will reveal? Occasionally it may be our destiny to act to change what caused them, so that others are not inconvenienced in the future.

Above all, we are pleased to learn from what happens and adjust our future actions accordingly. While few people choose to live in equatorial swamps, it is good to find ways of being happy and effective in as many of the Universe's infinite places and possibilities, as we can. To narrow down life to "home and away" areas is to trap ourselves in insecurity. If we travel with patient, kind and sensitive eyes, we will see the same rules apply everywhere and always feel at home. This is the way of liberation – the way of Zen.

Right: arriving in good time, relaxing into the pace of a delay (if it cannot be avoided) can bring many blessings.

WORKING TOGETHER

"I can wait, fast and work"
Siddhartha's recipe for material success.Siddhartha,
Herman Hesse

Below: usually, success at work is judged by outer displays of wealth – equity values, sales figures, turnover, size of salary, the house we live in, our car and other possessions.

Most of us find we can only care for those we love by spending the most productive and alive time of our days working away from them in an intensely competitive environment. To do so, most people need to acquire a wide range of special skills, qualifications, economic theories and techniques. Yet, the crucial rights and wrongs of what we do at work are usually left to our own value judgement. What works and succeeds, "brings home the bacon", is usually looked up to and followed. The successful person is the rich person. Poor people are failures, who need to learn how to be richer. Kind people help them do so.

Usually, success at work is judged by outer displays of wealth – equity values, sales figures, turnover, size of salary, the house we live in, our car and other possessions. The ability to select, hide or manipulate results, empire-build, and gain advantage by political pressure can create an unfair appearance of success. Because winning and possession are all important, arguments over the rules are commonplace – hence the power of certain kinds of lawyer and accountant. Things that are difficult to measure in money are disregarded.

With its constant drive to change and distort the "natural flow" and manipulate for reward, this modern world of work seems as alien as it could be from the way of Zen. Yet, this modern world of work just by existing is a part of the Tao. If it is done, it cannot be undone. Zen Buddhism does not care only for the good. It treats both the good and the bad appropriately. When we see our world of work as a part of the Tao, we start to live successfully in it.

Below: acting calmly, appropriately and efficiently is the secret of success.

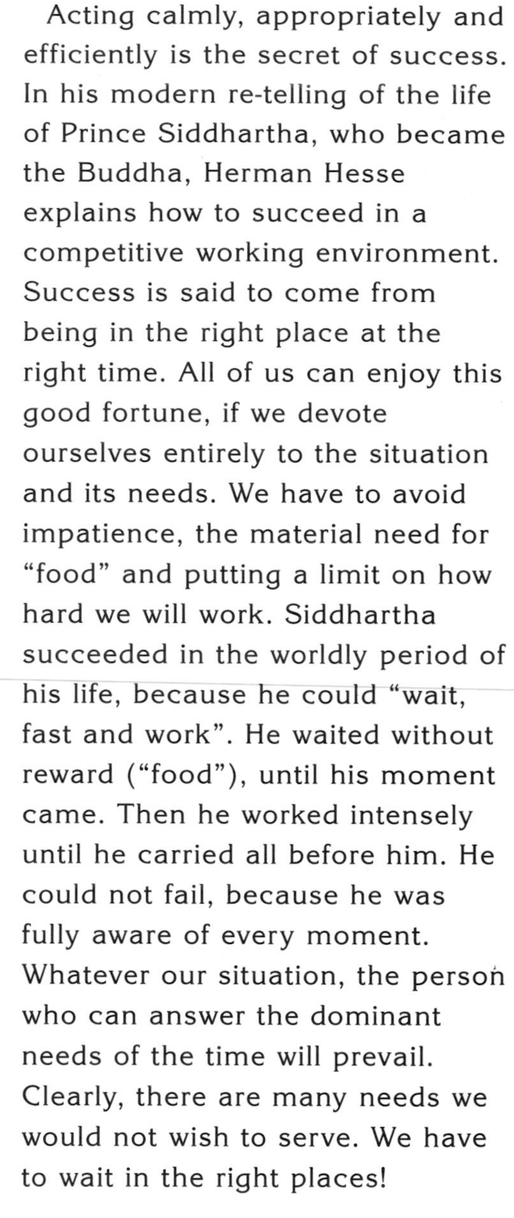

Acting calmly, appropriately and efficiently is the secret of success. In his modern re-telling of the life of Prince Siddhartha, who became the Buddha, Herman Hesse explains how to succeed in a competitive working environment. Success is said to come from being in the right place at the right time. All of us can enjoy this good fortune, if we devote ourselves entirely to the situation and its needs. We have to avoid impatience, the material need for "food" and putting a limit on how hard we will work. Siddhartha succeeded in the worldly period of his life, because he could "wait, fast and work". He waited without reward ("food"), until his moment came. Then he worked intensely until he carried all before him. He could not fail, because he was fully aware of every moment. Whatever our situation, the person who can answer the dominant needs of the time will prevail. Clearly, there are many needs we would not wish to serve. We have to wait in the right places!

Left: success is said to come from being in the right place at the right time. All of us can enjoy this good fortune, if we devote ourselves entirely to the situation and its needs.

Nor is this as heavy and absolute as it may first seem. The technique can be used on many levels. Whether we aspire to leadership, or just a pleasant everyday working experience, our destiny is in our own hands. The work environment offers many structures and opportunities. If we look selflessly at the needs of the work situation, act appropriately and compromise no further than we wish our time will come.

Which brings us back to our families. Our commitments should be balanced between them and our work. Who do we really want to be with? There is no benefit in denying what we love, to dedicate ourselves to something inappropriate. Nor is there happiness in denying love. We must be where we wish to be and accept what this involves. If our family needs demand it, we can survive with less material resources. Love and happiness can rest easily together in the most unpleasant situations. Waiting, fasting and working at the right times will lead to the opening up of the right opportunities.

When we do the right thing at the right time for the right reasons, people will love and support us and many kinds of wealth can pour in.

Far right: by balancing our work and family life appropriately we bring happiness to our world and to our own lives.

MONEY MATTERS

"The only security is insecurity.
If we can live comfortably with insecurity;
there is nothing we can lose.
So, we will always feel secure.
On the other hand, if we depend on security,
there is always the fear of losing it.
So we will always feel insecure."
Anon

In today's world the notion that "money is the root of all evil" seems to have become reversed. We tend to measure success and respectability from a person's ability to pay and prosper. Leaving commercial markets free of government interference to decide price and distribution matters is said to be the most efficient way to manage economies. Having money sets us free to choose where we wish to live and what we wish to do. Basing prices and availability on what people are willing to pay ensures efficiency and plentiful availability. Whether these assumptions are absolutely correct or not; it is certainly true that, to live satisfactorily in the modern world, we have to work within them.

As a result, how much money we have and how we protect and use it is very important. Few people nowadays would take a vow of poverty with any degree of confidence. To walk out into the world, with only the clothes on our backs, ready to beg for food, may be possible, but it is barely considered legal and certainly is not respectable. Paradoxically, this is much more so in the richest societies of the world, than it is in the poorest.

Then, there is the problem of never having enough. If we feel being rich is all-important, the dissatisfaction of seeing someone richer than ourselves is a constant frustration. To a pedestrian, any motorised transport is the height of luxury. To the proud motorist only a good modern car, with "all the trimmings" will do. Many of us look down on people, who drive old cars, live in poor neighbourhoods and dress themselves with "hand me downs". Appearance and image are paramount.

Because having the means to pay our way through life is so vital, we are open to a wide range of offers that claim to protect us from loss and the experience, even the appearance, of penury. To survive conveniently in most modern societies, several credit, debit and cash point cards are necessary. Then we feel the need to pay insurance premiums to protect ourselves against the possibility of losing these or our other possessions, commitments we cannot keep, or even liability for our own actions that go wrong. Yet, how can we ever feel secure in an increasingly criminal society? The richer we are, the more vulnerable we are to being attacked or robbed. Insurance policies cannot protect us, however much their premiums rise. Where is happiness, if we have to live in a state of general paranoia?

Left: to survive conveniently in most modern societies, several credit, debit and cash point cards are necessary.

Right: If we feel being rich is all-important, the dissatisfaction of seeing someone richer than ourselves is a constant frustration. To the proud motorist only a good modern car, with "all the trimmings" will do.

The main failing of the experience of living in the modern world is the attempt to grasp and hold on to pleasure, not only now, but also in the future. "I will always have enough to eat, if I have enough money." "Even if I lose all my money, I will be compensated." These are fruitless endeavours. For, as long as the mind is experiencing anxiety, any actions that are taken that fuel that anxiety are likely to make matters worse. Worried that the bank will fail, Mrs Jones keeps her money in the house. Worried that she may be robbed, Mrs Jones has an insurance policy. The insurers insist the money be kept in a locked safe. Worried about the honesty of the men from the security company, who fitted the safe, Mrs Jones stays awake all night. Seeing her fidget and look out of the window frequently through the night, a passing robber watches the house and enters and robs it, when she leaves the next morning. Worried that she did not lock the door properly, she returns, disturbs the robber and is lucky not to be killed. Does this experience confirm she was right to worry? Could she have avoided most of it?

According to Buddhism, greed, ignorance and hatred lie at the root of all our problems. For these three things to arise, there must be the delusion of attachment to something that will not last. It is obvious that the joy of eating ice cream will soon fade if we eat too much, or if we leave it to melt. It may not be so obvious that Mrs Jones' various reliances, outlined in the previous paragraph, were attempts to make the impermanent, permanent – even to guarantee its permanence.

In such a state of mind, we have to watch our step all the time. Everyone "may be the enemy, who will deprive us". In contrast, if we follow the path that opens up before us with alert minds, reveal ourselves modestly and deal appropriately with all eventualities, there is more chance we will pass through without incident. If problems occur, we will find friends.

Although the norm of today's world seems to be to achieve most things through money and the material possessions this brings, good friendships can and will work magical wonders. However we choose to live our lives, there are and always will be helpers on the way. The crucial thing is to have and show faith in the way that unfolds as we walk through life. The notion that the only really secure person is one that can live with insecurity is more than a play on words.

When we let fear fade away and accept and live with our insecurity, we open ourselves up to new friendships. Then we find there is a boundless community of support and supporters even in today's world. These are priceless beyond mere money. For, while money certainly matters, knowing where we stand and whom we stand with in the universe matters even more.

Below: the notion that the only really secure person is one that can live with insecurity is more than a play on words. When we let fear fade away we find there is a boundless community of support.

MASTERING MODERN TECHNOLOGY

"Not knowing how near the Truth is,
People seek it far away – what a pity!
They are like him who, in the midst of water,
Cries in thirst so imploringly."
Hakuin

For thousands of years, the only devices that gave people some strength in the face of nature were heavy and mechanical. We used winches and pulleys, simple levers, wheels and rollers to create all kinds of buildings, even pyramids and cathedrals. We built roads and sailed ships around the world. Such devices were solid and easy to see and understand. The development of steam power in the eighteenth century gave us a taste for the superhuman, but our machines became even larger, powerful and cumbersome. The more recent use of petroleum has been more efficient, but polluting in many ways and dependent on electricity and computing to fully develop.

Below: early mechanical devices were easy to see and understand

Indeed, it was only when we learned to produce and harness electricity that a seed change was possible in the life of humanity.

Early experiments suggested that electricity was too supple. It could run labour-saving devices, revolutionising our households, but did it have the raw power needed to drive heavy machinery? The ability to send messages and entertainment through the air, create light and ease the drudgery of life were novel and convenient, but not fundamental. Then people realised what great leaders had known all the time: that it is in the ability to see, know and communicate that the real power lies. The development of radar, television, computers and crucial linking devices such as the Internet are at the point of changing the physical and social structure of our lives. This change could be as fundamental as when humanity started to cultivate the land thousands of years ago.

Above: the harnessing of electrical power created a seed change in the life of humanity.

Left: today, the development of computers and crucial linking devices such as the Internet are at the point of changing the physical and social structure of our lives.

Right: this technological change could be as fundamental as when humanity started to cultivate the land thousands of years ago.

Below: older people living today may feel reasonably comfortable with an on/off switch, volume and tuning control, but button pressing from a remote control, toggling, menus and sub-menus can be very confusing.

It has all been so quick! Older people living today may feel reasonably comfortable with an on/off switch, volume and tuning control, but button pressing from a remote control, toggling, menus and sub-menus can be very confusing. Single keys that do different things, depending on what you pressed first, or how often you press them seem to defy logic. To those of us who see switches as things that turn machinery on and off, by causing electricity to flow, fear of pressing the wrong switch is paramount. "We may break it, or hurt ourselves. It is so complicated. I am too old. I will never learn". We should not allow such fears to form unnatural barriers to our living in the modern world. The solution is always close at hand, if we experiment without fear of the consequences.

Books and other people may help, but becoming intimately involved with the equipment and its controls is the way to find answers and overcome anxiety. It is very rare to break equipment by experimenting in this way. If we are lost, all we need to do is save as much as we can, then switch off and back on again. This nearly always brings us back to familiar territory. The experience of feeling "in control after all" is Zen-like "enlightenment" indeed!

Above: to a younger person born with a natural inclination to "dive in, fiddle and experiment", fear of electronic devices is not a consideration.

To a younger person born with a natural inclination to "dive in, fiddle and experiment", fear of electronic devices is not a consideration. The problem for this age group is not the complexity, but that "fiddling" is all there is to do. In recent years, the essence of computer games and television programme content has changed little. Nor has the structure and type of communication on the Internet developed greatly. Instead the focus of electronic development has been with bringing in new machinery, memory capacity, satellites, cables and other delivery devices. So, we have more and more channels and things to watch and find out about, but little or no real way of judging what is worth watching, or doing anything about what we are bombarded with.

Modern life seems to be putting more and more electronic barriers between us and other people. Telephone numbers become ever longer. Answering machines and automatic phone systems can be especially inconvenient. Pushing phone buttons to select a choice, even typing in an account number, may be reasonable. We may even accept that the service offered is a very popular bargain and settle down for a long wait. We leave the hands-free phone on the cradle and do something else. Then a real life operator will come on the line, ask what we want and put us back on hold – now with the phone in our hand! We may get used to the music, but never the interrupting voice, that constantly assures us "you are in a queue and will be dealt with very soon". We rarely are! Often officials we finally speak to can seem little more than an extension of the electronic system. They insist that our query cannot be answered, is against company policy, or "I will check up and phone you back very soon". They rarely do.

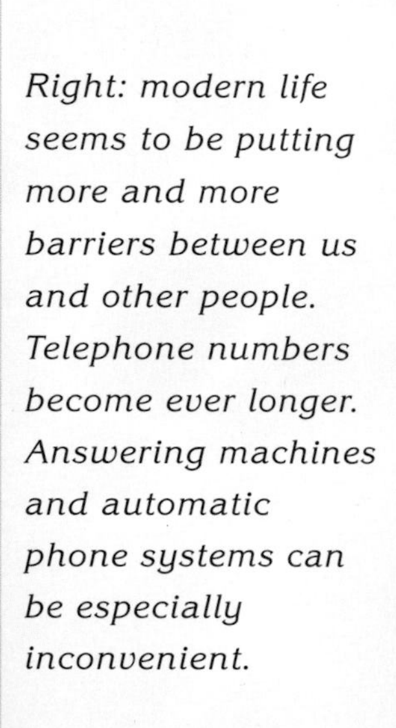

Right: modern life seems to be putting more and more barriers between us and other people. Telephone numbers become ever longer. Answering machines and automatic phone systems can be especially inconvenient.

It is now possible to shop on the Internet – even for groceries. Virtual reality software and holographic projection devices could make the experience of basket-filling pretty life-like. We may be able to visit, even sense the touch of our friends and relatives in other parts of the world, without leaving our room. Software that will type our words, even translate them into another language, machines that will obey our commands, aeroplanes and cars that drive themselves; all are either ready or in preparation.

In the Buddhist tradition, being entirely selfless and compassionately at one with the here and now develops very special yogic powers. These special powers are said to enable the seeing and moving over vast distances, becoming very small, taking many forms, remaining young, penetrating barriers, having power over treasures. If such powers are misused for self-indulgence, or to dominate others, the fall from grace is sudden, deep and extremely painful.

The possibilities of modern technology suggest humanity has reached a stage of such responsibility. If we use and develop its power with the same care as we use a knife or a car in our everyday lives, it could have many positive benefits. If we use it to enrich our lives and those of other people, all will be well. If we use it to exchange ideas and develop values to guide our new circumstances, the place of modern technology will be clear and our lives all the better for it.

Above: it is now possible to shop on the Internet, for anything we could possibly want.

ENJOYING THE PAST, PRESENT AND FUTURE

"Everything in the Universe comes out of Nothing.
Follow the nothingness of the Tao,
And you can be like it, not needing anything,
But seeing the wonder and root of everything."
Tao Te Ching

Below: even when we find ourselves in perfect surroundings, the question of whether it will last causes its own problems.

Sea-like surges of sensuous sound; enchanting vibrant colours; aromas that dance teasingly upon our nostrils; the touch of soft silk upon our bodies; eating a perfectly cooked and presented meal: how can there be anything more fortunate than finding and living in a perfect place with all its attendant pleasures?

By asking this question we create a problem that did not previously exist. For it is at this point of asking and increasingly after, that our minds begin to worry. As soon as we move on from pure experience to measuring and maintaining it, we express doubt and dissatisfaction. If what was happening was absolutely perfect, then how could we have room to question its impermanence? If we need to guarantee our present pleasure will continue, it cannot be perfect. The problem is never the experience itself, but our dissatisfied state of mind about it. It is quite clear that sensual experience, while wonderful at times, cannot guarantee happiness, or the lack of it sadness. If we visit an "eat as much as you can" restaurant, we will soon see how limited food is in its ability to give happiness, however large the appetite.

Left: advertisers are constantly encouraging us to need and consume, using seductive images of far-off places and idyllic surroundings, promising that they will change our lives for the better.

So, it is not sensual satisfaction, its source, or the lack of either, that makes us happy or unhappy. Rather, it is our state of mind about the reliability of a pleasing experience. Yet, advertisements in today's world are constantly encouraging us to need and consume. It is suggested that to go on holiday to that place, to drink or eat that product or wear those clothes will dramatically change our state of mind for the better. Are these advertisers, who also fund so much of our sport and general entertainment, at the same time sowing the seeds of our continual dissatisfaction? They are not entirely to blame. They may be tempting us by playing on our ignorance and weaknesses, but, while we have mental freedom, we make the decisions and have to accept the responsibility.

Right: information brought to us on mass through modern technology has been influencing us on mass since the 1960s

Below: the sports we support and entertainments we prefer are only financially successful, because we watch and spend money in such substantial amounts on them.

Indeed, if we are willing to step aside from fighting for personal benefit all the time, the mass of information, human understanding and electric spontaneity offered by modern information and entertainment facilities does provide all we need to make correct decisions. The Vietnam War was finally ended by public pressure, because of the close media coverage of what was happening. Since then, it has been difficult for the USA to go to war in the same way.

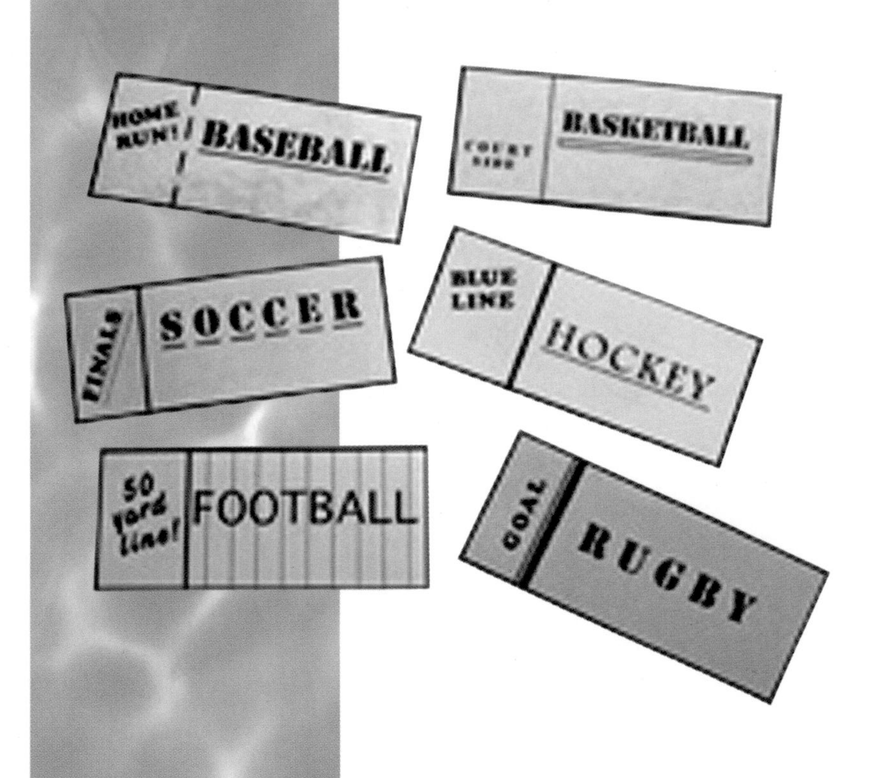

The sports we support and entertainments we prefer are only financially successful, because we watch and spend money in such substantial amounts on them. If we could let go of attachment to our team winning, we would certainly be happier. So would most other people. For in any elimination competition only a small number can attain the fleeting happiness of total success. Some supporters are content to enjoy the hope – so long as it lasts – and even the final defeat, when it comes. It is possible to take a Zen approach to supporting a team. We could train ourselves to celebrate the losing of a lover, or being too ill to go on holiday.

The quotation from the Tao Te Ching that heads this chapter offers a very different and more fertile way of looking at and experiencing happiness in any situation. Since there is a reaction to every action, word, or thought, by taking a position, or having an expectation, we become a prejudiced participant. When we want something from a situation, it is almost certain that we will not see it clearly as it is. We will not appreciate it on its own merit. To fight for what we want and force a truth on people they are not ready to accept is to court embarrassment and failure. To look for how situations could – or should – be is to guarantee disappointment. To see things as they are is to leave space for something really special to occur and to be open to an experience of the wondrous magic of the Universe.

Paradoxically, because such a state of mind is almost entirely focussed on the present, it is eminently suited to put the past and future in perspective. When we are fully aware of what is happening, we are more likely to know what caused the situation and what will happen next. Seeing things clearly as they are releases us from responsibility for the past and fear of the future. For, by being fully aware of the present, we can know and flow willingly into the future.

Looking at life from a Zen perspective frees us from: fear of the consequences; worrying about things that have not and might never happen; what we think are our social and family obligations; creating an acceptable image; even being condemned as a failure. This does not mean it frees us from our responsibility for others. Zen is a part of the Mahayana strand of Buddhism. This emphasises that enlightenment cannot be complete until our minds are single-mindedly focused on the need for all creatures to be liberated from the suffering of sense-based attachment. Taking a Zen perspective focuses us clearly on things as they really are and clarifies our role in helping others. This enables us to know and celebrate the Universe as it is.

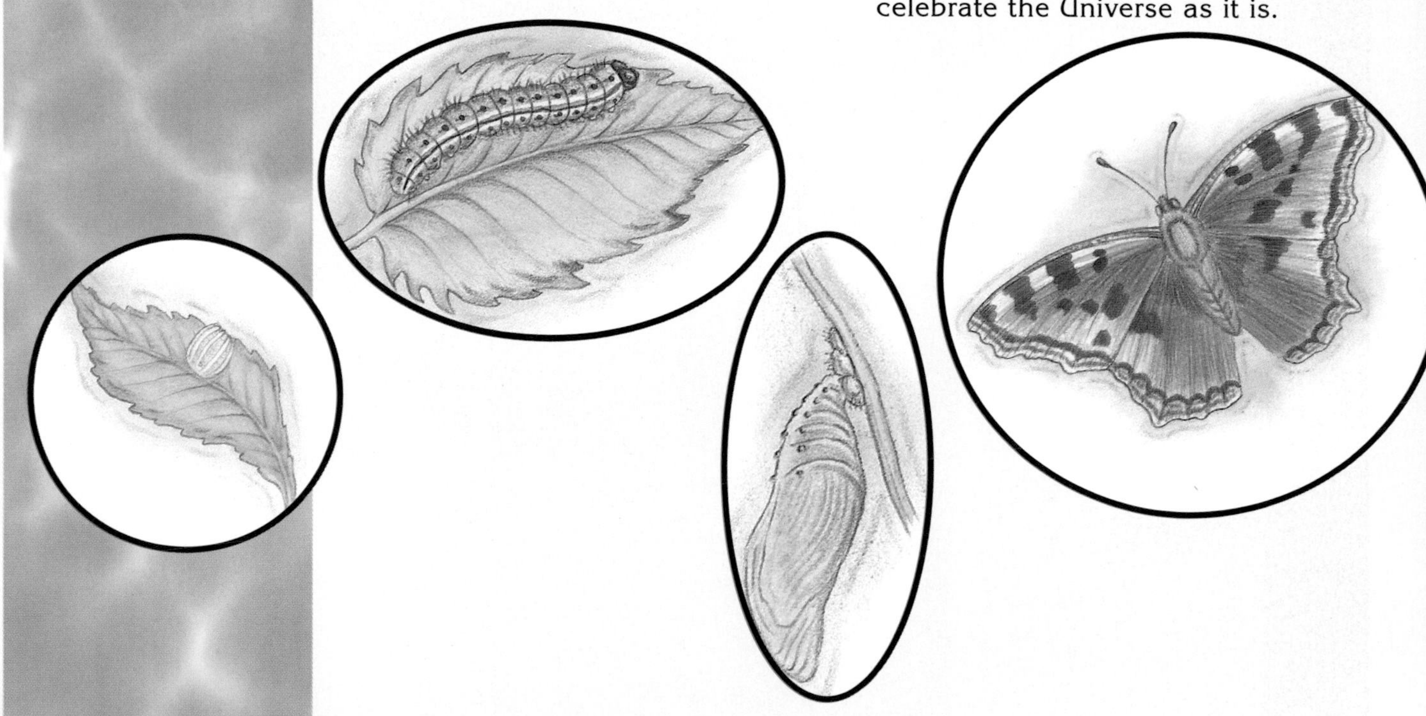

Enlightenment is often compared to our method of walking comfortably. To cover the entire surface of the earth with leather would clearly be impossible, but, by wearing just one pair of sandals, wherever we walk is covered in leather. If it is not us who are enlightened now, how can we talk about, or judge the achievements of others? How can we say what should have happened in the past, or should or should not happen in the future? If we live with full awareness and concentration in every moment of the present, we will be in a state of constant awareness and happiness that will never cease. If not us, who? If not now, when?

Left: to cover the entire surface of the earth with leather would clearly be impossible, but, by wearing just one pair of sandals, wherever we walk is covered in leather.

INDEX

INDEX